SCIENCE HIGHLIGHTS

1500–1700

REVOLUTIONS IN SCIENCE

Charlie Samuels

Gareth Stevens
Publishing

Please visit our Web site www.garethstevens.com. For a free color catalog of all our high-quality books, call toll free 1-800-542-2595 or fax 1-877-542-2596.

Library of Congress Cataloging-in-Publication Data
Samuels, Charlie, 1961-
Revolutions in science : 1500-1700 / Charlie Samuels.
    p. cm. — (Science highlights)
Includes bibliographical references and index.
ISBN 978-1-4339-4142-9 (lib. bdg. : alk. paper)
ISBN 978-1-4339-4143-6 (pbk. : alk. paper)
ISBN 978-1-4339-4144-3 (6-pack : alk. paper)
1. Science—History—16th century—Juvenile literature. 2. Science—History—17th century—Juvenile literature. I. Title.
Q125.2.S26 2011
509'.03—dc22

                             2010009082

Published in 2011 by
Gareth Stevens Publishing
111 East 14th Street, Suite 349
New York, NY 10003

© 2011 The Brown Reference Group Ltd.

For Gareth Stevens Publishing:
Art Direction: Haley Harasymiw
Editorial Direction: Kerri O'Donnell

For The Brown Reference Group Ltd:
Editorial Director: Lindsey Lowe
Managing Editor: Tim Cooke
Children's Publisher: Anne O'Daly
Design Manager: David Poole
Designer: Kim Browne
Picture Manager: Sophie Mortimer
Production Director: Alastair Gourlay

Picture Credits
Front Cover: Thinkstock: Photos.com

Inside: iStockphoto: Jacus 20, Dariusz Sas 6; **Shutterstock:** 11cl, Arogant 7br, Awe Inspiring Images 33, Laurent Dambies 16, Janaka Dharmasena 12, 13tc, 14tr, 15, Dyonna 24, Daniel Gale 43, Leigh 13c, Lofoto 36, Lolloj 14cl, Andrei Merkulov 19c, Ho Philip 27t, Kenneth V. Pilson 10, Triff 5, Paul Van Eykebem 39, Yakobchuk Vasyl 32; **Thinkstock:** 7tl, 8tr, 9, 11tc, 17, 18, 19tr, 21tl, 21br, 23, 25, 28, 29, 30, 31t, 34, 37tl, 37cr, 38, 41, 42, 45.

All Artworks Brown Reference Group

The Brown Reference Group has made every attempt to contact the copyright holders. If anyone has any information please contact info@brownreference.com

Manufactured in the United States of America
1 2 3 4 5 6 7 8 9 12 11 10

CPSIA compliance information: Batch #CS10GS: For further information contact Gareth Stevens, New York, New York at 1-800-542-2595.

Contents

Introduction

The period from the start of the 16th century to the start of the 18th century saw a huge expansion in what people understood about themselves and their world.

The growth of learning had its roots in changes that had begun in the late Middle Ages. Economic growth in Europe brought increased trade, bigger towns and cities, and the exchange of ideas as more people traveled further. One result was the Renaissance, literally a "rebirth" of classical learning, which spurred a new spirit of inquiry into many subjects. The artist Leonardo da Vinci devised complex machines, while astronomers Nicolaus Copernicus and Galileo Galilei both denied the accepted belief that the sun went around Earth. Their theories were among the many new ideas that circulated rapidly throughout Europe thanks to the development of cheaper forms of printing.

The Age of Reason

The 17th century was dominated by thinkers such as Galileo and the English scientist Isaac Newton. But these men were experimenters as well as thinkers. They used observation and experiment to formulate laws about the workings of the universe that are still accepted today. In doing so, they laid the foundations of modern scientific methods.

About This Book

This book uses timelines to describe the vast upheavals that took place in scientific knowledge from about 1500 to about 1700. A continuous timeline of the whole period runs along the bottom of all the pages. Its entries are color-coded to indicate the different fields of science to which the developments belong. Each chapter also has a subject-specific timeline, which runs vertically down the side of the page.

Advances in scientific methods, including better telescopes and microscopes, revealed unseen details—from the surface of the moon to the shape of bacteria. ↓

Printing

Printing originated in China in about the ninth century. By 1045, Bi Sheng had invented movable type made of baked clay and within 10 years was printing books with it.

← Movable type can be made into words and pages, then taken apart and reused.

TIMELINE
1500–1510

1500 English printer Wynkyn de Worde sets up a printing press in Fleet Street, London, which establishes it as the city's future newspaper center.

1500 Portuguese navigator Pedro Cabral discovers the coast of Brazil and claims it for Portugal.

1500   1502   1504

KEY:

Astronomy and Math

Physical and Life Sciences

Technology

1500 Chinese inventor Wan Hu tries to make a flying machine by tying 45 rockets to the back of a chair; the device explodes, killing him.

1502 German clockmaker Peter Henlein makes the first spring-driven pocket clock (watch).

1503 Spanish military engineer Pedro Navarro explodes a series of mines under castles at Naples, beginning a new form of land warfare.

Johannes Gutenberg was the first European to use movable type.

The first Chinese printers made paper money and books, with each page of characters carved from a single block of wood to make the printing "plate." The same technology dominated European printing until the middle of the 15th century.

Printing from cast-metal type began in Korea in the 1390s. In 1403, the Korean king Taejong authorized the casting of metal type in bronze. Other printers adopted woodcuts for printing, often carving the type for whole pages out of a single piece of wood. That had the disadvantage that every new page had to be carved from scratch. It would be more efficient to be able to arrange a set of standard characters to form sentences and paragraphs. However, there are thousands of different characters in the Chinese language. In 1313, the Chinese printer Wang Chen had to use more than 50,000 movable wooden

Timeline

1395 Cast metal type used in Korea

1403 Bronze type used in Korea

1438 Wooden blocks used by Koster for printing

1442 Printing press established by Gutenberg

1455 World's first book printed using movable metal type

1474 First book printed in the English language

← Gutenberg adapted a wine press to squeeze the paper against the inked type.

1507 The Italian architect Fra Giovanni Giocondo constructs the Pont Notre Dame in Paris to connect the North Bank of the Seine River to the island of La Cité, site of Notre Dame Cathedral.

1506   1508   1510

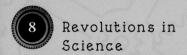

Letterpress Printing

In letterpress printing, characters are raised, mirror-image letters. They are set as text and locked into a frame, then inked with a roller. Paper is pressed against the type. When the paper is peeled off the type, it retains the printed image.

Printed letter on paper

Raised letter on metal base

characters to print his *Treatise on Agriculture.*

By 1438, Dutch printer Laurens Koster of Haarlem is thought to have used movable wooden blocks for printing. The blocks were far more useful for European languages, which only had 26 characters—the letters of the alphabet—and various punctuation marks, such as periods and commas.

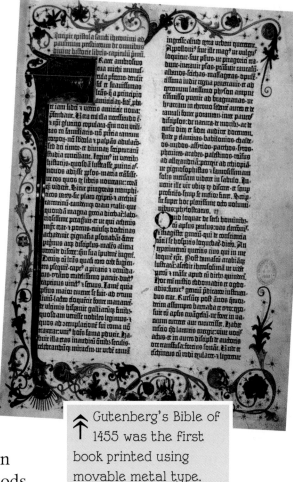

↑ Gutenberg's Bible of 1455 was the first book printed using movable metal type.

Johannes Gutenberg

Metal type was reinvented in Europe by the German inventor Johannes Gutenberg (c.1400–68) in the 1440s. Gutenberg brought together the ideas of making copper molds in which to cast the type, a suitable low-melting

TIMELINE 1510–1520

1513 Swiss artist Urs Graf introduces the technique of metal etching.

1515 The wheel-lock pistol is introduced in Germany.

1510   1512   1514

1513 Spanish explorer Vasco Balboa crosses the Isthmus of Panama and sees the Pacific Ocean.

KEY:

Astronomy and Math

Physical and Life Sciences

Technology

lead alloy to do the casting, a special oil-based printing ink, and—most importantly—a printing press that would squeeze the paper against the inked printing plates. For this purpose, Gutenberg adapted the screw press, which was already in common use in southern Europe for crushing the juice out of grapes to make wine. (Early East Asian printers did not use a printing press. Instead, they placed the paper on the inked type and used a brush or a roller to push the paper and the type into contact.)

Gutenberg set up his first printing press in about 1442 in Strasbourg, France, but around 1450 he returned to his hometown of Mainz, Germany. He established a press using money put up by his commercial partners, German businessman Johann Fust and German printer Peter Schöffer. Gutenberg's first book—and the world's first book ever to be printed using movable metal type—was a Latin Bible, which he produced in 1455 with his new partner, Konrad Humery. It is sometimes known as the Forty-Two Line Bible, because its Latin text was printed in 42-line columns. Like other publications of that time, Gutenberg's Bible had no page numbers, no title page, and nothing to indicate who had published it. The first printed book in Europe to carry the name of

↑ Early books were highly valuable, so the pages were bound into protective covers.

1517 Italian physician Girolamo Fracastoro proposes that fossils are the petrified remains of once-living organisms.

1518 Smallpox reaches the Americas, carried by European explorers and settlers.The disease decimates native peoples with no immunity to it.

1516   1518   1520

1515 German astronomer Johannes Schöner makes the first globe to include the name "America."

1518 English physician Thomas Linacre founds the Royal College of Physicians in London.

1519 Portuguese navigator Ferdinand Magellan observes the Magellanic clouds, two small galaxies that are the nearest to our own galaxy, the Milky Way.

Berta etas mundi

Expeditio in Bohemos hereticos facta temporibus Sigismundi

[Latin text of the Nuremberg Chronicle page]

The Nuremberg *Chronicle* appeared in 1493, printed from a single plate rather than movable type.

its printer was a book of psalms produced in 1457 by Schöffer. It was also the first book to be printed in two colors. In about 1475, Schöffer, who by then had gone into business on his own, began using steel dies in order to stamp out the copper molds for typecasting.

The Spread of Printing

Printing presses soon began to appear in other parts of Europe. The first press in Italy, at Subiaco near Rome, was established in 1465, and by 1470, the university in Paris, France, had its own press. In 1471, German astronomer and mathematician Regiomontanus (Johannes Müller) set up a press at his Nuremberg observatory for printing astronomical tables, which detailed the movements of the stars and planets.

Metal-type printing was introduced into England by William Caxton (c.1422–c.1491). In 1474, Caxton, working together with the Flemish calligrapher Colard Mansion, had been the first person to print a book in the English language, which he had completed while living in Bruges, Belgium. Called *Recuyell of the Historyes of Troye*, the account of the Trojan

TIMELINE
1520–1530

1522 The expedition of Portuguese sailor Ferdinand Magellan completes the first circumnavigation of the globe (Magellan himself was killed a year earlier).

1525 German mathematician Christoff Rudolf writes the first German book on algebra.

1520   1522   1524

KEY:

Astronomy and Math

Physical and Life Sciences

Technology

1520 Returning Spanish voyagers introduce turkeys and corn (maize) from America to Europe.

1522 In China, potters make fine, pale-blue porcelain in the Chia-Ching period.

1525 The Swiss-born alchemist Paracelsus introduces laudanum (tincture of opium) as an anesthetic in medicine.

Wars in ancient Greece had been translated from the original French by Caxton himself. He printed another of his own translations from French (*The Game and Playe of the Chesse*) a year later. Caxton returned to England in 1476 and set up a

 William Caxton presents one of his books to the English king Edward IV.

Early illustrations were woodcuts, like this 1485 drawing from *The Canterbury Tales*.

printing press in London a year later. In 1481, he published the first illustrated book in English. His Caxton Press published more than 100 works over 15 years. Many of the books were translations made by Caxton himself, mainly from original texts in French.

The Spread of Printing

Printing with moveable type soon spread across Europe. Printers set up workshops in major cities. There was no copyright law, so many simply printed their own editions of other people's books. Usually, printers did not bind books. The customer bought a collection of loose pages and arranged to have them put into whatever covers they chose. The easy availability of cheaper books helped to spread ideas, such as those of the Protestant Reformation.

1526 Spanish explorer Francisco Pizarro enters South America and reaches Peru for the first time.

1530 Italian physician Girolamo Fracastoro observes and describes the disease syphilis among sailors returning from America.

1526   1528   1530

1525 The fusée, a conical pulley that equalizes the pull of a clock's spring as it winds down, is first used in spring-powered clocks.

1527 German astronomer Petrus Apianus includes Pascal's triangle in one of his publications.

Leonardo da Vinci

Leonardo was an Italian artist, architect, sculptor, and engineer. He made many contributions to science, mainly to anatomy and the design of various mechanisms.

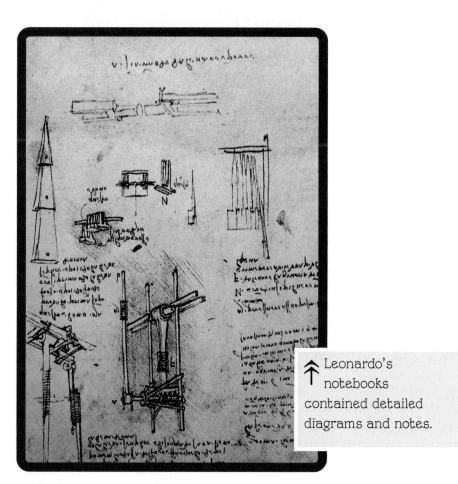

⬆ Leonardo's notebooks contained detailed diagrams and notes.

TIMELINE
1530–1540

1530 Swiss cleric Otto Brunfels and German artist Hans Weiditz produce *Living Portraits of Plants*, a book that begins the modern era of descriptive botany.

1533 Dutch mathematician Regnier Gemma Frisius gives the first published account of the use of triangulation in surveying and mapmaking.

1530   1532   1534

1531 German cartographer Sebastian Münster publishes *Horologiographia*, which describes the construction of sundials.

1534 French navigator Jacques Cartier makes his first voyage to the Gulf of St. Lawrence.

KEY:

▢ Astronomy and Math

▢ Physical and Life Sciences

▢ Technology

Leonardo was born in Vinci, near Florence in northern Italy, in 1452. At the age of 16, he became an apprentice to artist Andrea del Verrocchio. Leonardo made a series of detailed drawings when preparing sketches for his paintings. Most of our information about Leonardo comes from his detailed notebooks.

↑ These designs for field weapons show a device similar to a tank (bottom right).

The Artist's Life

In 1482, Leonardo moved to Milan to work for Ludovico Sforza, later duke of Milan. In 1499, he returned to work in Florence for the soldier, engineer, and architect Cesare Borgia. He painted a series of masterpieces, such as *The Last Supper* and the *Mona Lisa.* After working in Milan again and for three years in Rome, he went to Amboise, France, under the patronage of King Francis I (reigned 1515–1547), with the title of "first painter, architect, and engineer to the king." The artist remained in France for the rest of his days.

Timeline

1452 Leonardo is born in Vinci

1468 Apprenticed to Verrocchio

1482 Moves to Milan to work for Sforza

1499 Goes to Florence

1502 Works for Cesare Borgia

1506 Returns to Milan to work for Louis XII

1513 Moves to Rome

1516 Goes to Amboise, France

1519 Leonardo dies in Amboise

← Leonardo da Vinci was one of the most versatile men of his time. He left a legacy of paintings, drawings, and notebooks that show an exceptional range of skills.

LEONARDO DAVINCI

1536 On his second voyage across the Atlantic, Jacques Cartier claims Canada for France.

1540 French surgeon Ambrose Paré makes artificial limbs with joints.

1536   1538   1540

1535 The diving bell comes into use in Europe for working on bridge foundations and shipwrecks underwater.

1537 Italian mathematician Niccolò Tartaglia invents the gunner's quadrant for aiming cannons.

Leonardo and Biology

Leonardo wanted to understand how the human body worked, partly so that he could draw it better. He watched dead bodies being dissected and made precise anatomical diagrams of the muscles and the internal organs.

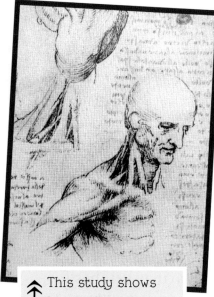

↑ This study shows Leonardo exploring how tendons and muscles work.

Throughout his long working life, Leonardo made sketches and plans of an amazing range of fortifications, civil engineering schemes, and mechanisms. He described pulleys and belt drives to transmit power, a treadle-operated lathe, a paddle-wheel boat, and a machine for grinding and polishing glass lenses. He invented instruments for measuring the speed of a ship and for measuring the force of the wind. Starting with a design by Roman architect Marcus Vitruvius Pollio (b. 70 B.C.), he drew up plans for an odometer, a mechanical device to measure the distance traveled by a vehicle. He designed pumps, mechanized vehicles, and even a digging machine for excavating canals. From watching birds in flight, he designed an ornithopter, a man-powered, heavier-than-air flying machine with flapping wings. (It could never work because a human being could not possibly produce enough power.) There were also impractical

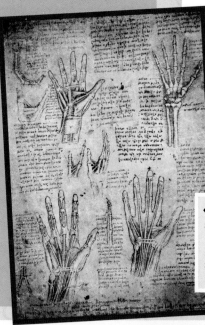

← Leonardo made these sketches to learn about how the hand works.

TIMELINE 1540–1550

KEY:

- Astronomy and Math
- Physical and Life Sciences
- Technology

1540 Italian metallurgist Vannoccio Biringuccio describes a pedal-powered machine used for boring cannon barrels.

1541 Austrian astronomer and mathematician Rheticus (Georg Joachim von Lauchen) publishes a set of trigonometrical tables.

1542 French physician Jean Fernel explains the condition appendicitis.

1543 Polish astronomer Nicolaus Copernicus describes his idea of a sun-centered universe.

1544 German cartographer Sebastian Münster publishes a book on world geography called *Cosmographia Universalis*.

1540   1542   1544

designs for a tortoise-shaped tank, a submarine, and a helicopter. His 1485 drawing of a pyramid-shaped parachute was more practical, and he is even thought to have made some small model parachutes and to have tested them.

Although he was an exceptional practical engineer, Leonardo did not understand mechanics in any theoretical way (perhaps because he never really learned math), and many of his views on science differed little from the teachings of Greek scientist and philosopher Aristotle (384–322 B.C.) 18 centuries earlier. Nevertheless, his wide-ranging talents spanning the arts and sciences made him the true Renaissance man. When Leonardo died in 1519, his lifelong friend and fellow painter Francesco Melzi (1493–1570) carefully gathered up his paintings, papers, and models made of wood and metal. However, after Melzi's death, many were lost or destroyed. Today only about 7,000 of the original 13,000 pages of notes have survived, but they are more than enough to testify to Leonardo's genius.

↑ This 1503 drawing shows an imagined flying machine that resembles a helicopter.

Could Leonardo Fly?

Leonardo made sketches of a number of flying machines, although no one knows if he ever tried to build any of them. One resembled a helicopter; another was a pyramid-shaped parachute. There were also machines with flapping wings that copied the flight of birds. Most probably would not have worked: they were too heavy or required more power than the human body can produce.

1545 The French mint introduces a screw press for making coins.

1546 English textile manufacturer William Stumpe sets up a weaving works housing 30 looms and employing 500 people.

1550 French surgeon Ambrose Paré begins the practice of tying off arteries with ligatures during surgery.

1546   1548   1550

1546 Italian physician Girolamo Fracastoro suggests that germs are the cause of disease.

Copernicus

"Finally we shall place the Sun himself at the center of the Universe." (Copernicus: *De Revolutionibus Orbium Coelestium*)

➤➤ Nicolaus Copernicus spent a lifetime contemplating the heavens.

TIMELINE
1550–1560

KEY:

- Astronomy and Math
- Physical and Life Sciences
- Technology

1551 English mathematician Leonard Digges invents the theodolite for measuring angles and levels during surveying.

1555 French-born printer Christophe Plantin sets up a print works in Antwerp, Belgium. Some of his type designs are still in use today.

1550 Swiss naturalist Konrad von Gesner begins his *Historia Animalium. Animals, Birds,* and *Fish* appear between 1551 and 1558.

1552 Italian anatomist Bartolomeo Eustachio identifies the Eustachian tubes from the middle ear to the throat.

1550   1552   1554

← This map shows the solar system according to Copernicus's ideas.

B orn Mikolaj Kopernik in Poland in 1473, Nicolaus Copernicus changed his name to the familiar version when he was a student. Copernicus' early studies included astronomy, Latin, mathematics, geography, philosophy, Greek, and canon law. The latter led to his appointment as canon of Frauenburg Cathedral in Poland, a position he held for the rest of his life. During the early 1500s, he was granted leave to study medicine at the University of Padua in Italy. But astronomy remained his passion.

The Ptolemaic Universe

Astronomy was still based on the observations of the ancient Greeks Aristotle and Ptolemy and the writings of English mathematician Johannes de Sacrobosco (d. c.1256). All assumed that Earth was the center of the

1556 French monk André Thevet introduces tobacco seeds to Europe from Brazil.

1556   1558   1560

1555 German miners use trucks running on rails, some of which are pushed by hand.

1556 *De Re Metallica* by German mineralogist Georgius Agricola is published after its author's death. It describes the formation of minerals and has information about mining and metal smelting.

Whose Idea Was It?

Copernicus was not the first to propose that the planets orbit the sun. The Greek astronomer Aristarchus of Samos suggested the idea in the third century B.C. And in 1425, the German cleric Nicholas of Cusa suggested not only that the Earth orbited the sun, but that space was infinite and that stars were other suns. Cusa believed that our knowledge was limited. There was so much to know, he thought, that trying to understand it all was like trying to see the corners on a circle.

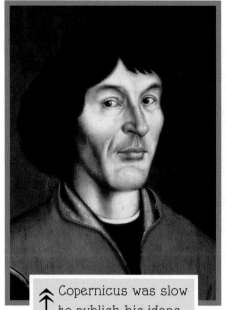

Copernicus was slow to publish his ideas because he feared the reaction of the Church.

universe and that the sun, moon, and planets revolved around it. Ptolemy believed in the perfection of the heavens: he proposed various reasons why the orbits of the celestial bodies were elliptical or oval rather than perfectly circular.

Evolving a Theory

Copernicus realized that many of the problems inherent in Ptolemy's system would disappear if one accepted that Earth moved around the sun. In 1514, he began distributing copies of a handwritten book, in which he laid out the principles of the heliocentric, or sun-centered, universe, including the suggestion that the apparent rotation of the stars and that seasonal movements of the sun are caused by the rotation of Earth on its axis and its movement around the sun. The book became known as the *Little Commentary*. It contained no detailed mathematics, and Copernicus did not even put his name to it. He was saving the details for what he called his "larger work."

TIMELINE
1560–1570

1561 Flemish engineer Pieter Breughel invents a mechanical dredger.

1563 The first potatoes are introduced to England from the Americas.

1560　　　　　1562　　　　　1564

1562 English navigator John Hawkins made his first visit to the West Indies, mainly to trade slaves from West Africa.

KEY:

- Astronomy and Math
- Physical and Life Sciences
- Technology

Copernicus did not complete his great book *De Revolutionibus Orbium Coelestium* (*On the Revolutions of the Heavenly Orbs*) until 1530. Being conscious that the Church taught that Earth was the center of God's creation, he allowed the manuscript to be read only by a few scientists.

Copernicus' student, Rheticus, persuaded him to publish the book and took the manuscript to Nürnberg to be printed. But the printer was uncomfortable with the implications of a sun-centered universe. He replaced Copernicus' preface to the book with one stating that, in truth, Earth is stationary and that the assumption that it moved around the sun was a device to make the calculations in the book simpler. It seems highly unlikely that Copernicus would have approved this addition, but he probably never got to read it—by the time the book was published, he was on his deathbed.

↑ Pope Leo X, who commissioned Copernicus to revise the calendar, oversees the burning of books that rejected Church teaching.

⇐ Stamps from the mid-20th century mark the contribution Copernicus made to astronomy.

1567 Italian architect Bartolomeo Ammanati builds the Santa Trinità Bridge, with an elliptical arch, over the Arno River in Florence, Italy.

1569 Flemish mapmaker Gerardus Mercator introduces the Mercator map projection for showing the spherical Earth on a flat piece of paper.

1566

1568

1570

1567 On a third voyage to the West Indies, John Hawkins is accompanied by English explorer Francis Drake.

1570 Italian architect Andrea Palladio publishes *Four Books on Architecture*, which describes the use of wooden trusses for bridge design.

Galileo Galilei

Galileo, as he is generally known, was a scientist who made fundamental contributions to astronomy, mathematics, and physics.

⟶ Galileo made a thermometer from vessels holding different liquids.

TIMELINE
1570–1580

1571 Flemish cartographer Abraham Ortelius publishes the first compendium of maps (the word "atlas" is not used until 1585).

1573 Italian anatomist Costanzo Varoli describes the optic nerves.

1573 Danish astronomer Tycho Brahe describes a new supernova in the constellation Cassiopeia.

1570   1572   1574

1573 English sailor Humphrey Cole devises a way to measure a ship's speed by tying a knotted rope to a log, throwing it overboard, and counting how many knots are dragged out in an allotted time.

KEY:

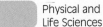

Astronomy and math

Physical and Life Sciences

Technology

Galileo gained fame by demonstrating his telescope to Italian high society.

Timeline

1582 Constancy of pendulum's swing

1602 Law of falling bodies

1610 Observes four of Jupiter's moons

1611 First views sunspots

1633 Condemned by the Inquisition

G alileo was born in Pisa in northern Italy, and educated in Florence and Pisa. He did not get a degree but began working as a teacher. His reputation spread, and in 1589 he became professor of mathematics at Pisa without any formal qualifications. He moved to Padua in 1592 and taught there until 1610.

Observation and Experiment

In 1582, in Pisa Cathedral, Galileo noticed the regular swings of a lamp in a draft. He made his own simple pendulum—like the swinging lamp—with a weight on a length of string, and then timed its swings using the beat of his pulse. He found that the time of each swing depended only on the length of the string, not the size of the weight. He suggested that a pendulum could be used to measure time, and pendulums were, in fact, used later to regulate mechanical clocks.

➤➤ Galileo made major contributions to astronomy, math, and physics.

1576 Englishman Robert Norman describes and measures magnetic dip, the downward tilt of a compass needle in Earth's magnetic field.

1580 Italian botanist and physician Prospero Alpini distinguishes between male and female flowers.

1576   1578   1580

1576 Danish astronomer Tycho Brahe establishes a purpose-built observatory on the island of Hven in the Baltic Sea.

The Speed of Falling Objects

When Galileo dropped two cannon balls from the Leaning Tower, they fell at the same speed and hit the ground together. He tried to show that they had a constant acceleration (the rate at which speed changes.) The diagram shows the results if he could have measured acceleration. As an object falls farther, it moves faster, but the acceleration is constant: 32 feet (9.8 m) per second per second, which is now known as the acceleration of free fall.

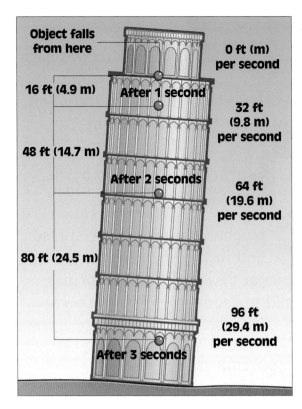

Object falls from here

After 1 second — 16 ft (4.9 m) — 0 ft (m) per second

32 ft (9.8 m) per second

48 ft (14.7 m)

After 2 seconds — 64 ft (19.6 m) per second

80 ft (24.5 m)

96 ft (29.4 m) per second

After 3 seconds

↑ Galileo's experiment showed how objects accelerate at a constant rate.

Since the time of the Greeks, people thought that the speed at which an object falls depends on its weight, so a heavier object would fall faster. Galileo put the idea to the test in about 1602. He is said to have dropped two cannonballs of different weight from the Leaning Tower of Pisa and showed that they hit the ground at the same time.

Galileo and Astronomy

The development of the telescope in the early 1600s stimulated Galileo's interest in astronomy. He made telescopes of his own and pointed them at the moon. He made drawings recording the moon's mountains and craters at different times during the month. He then

TIMELINE
1580–1590

KEY:
- Astronomy and math
- Physical and Life Sciences
- Technology

1580   1582   1584

1580 English explorer Francis Drake completes a circumnavigation of the globe.

1583 Italian botanist and physician Andrea Cesalpino devises a system of classifying plants by their structure.

1584 Italian philosopher and monk Giordano Bruno suggests a theory that the universe is infinite.

→ Galileo's 1632 book about the universe was banned by the Catholic church.

studied Jupiter, and in 1610 announced that the planet had four moons of its own. A year later, he aimed his telescope at the sun and noted that sometimes small black spots moved slowly across the sun's disk. The movement of sunspots showed him that the sun is rotating slowly on its axis.

Galileo became convinced that the sun is at the center of the solar system, a theory published in 1543 by Polish astronomer Nicolaus Copernicus. But the idea went against the teachings of Aristotle, who believed in an Earth-centered universe. It was also against the teachings of the Roman Catholic church. Church officials asked Galileo not to spread the idea, but in 1632 he published it in a book, which was banned. In 1633, he was arrested by the Inquisition, taken to Rome, and under threat of torture, made to recant his views.

Under House Arrest

Old and in failing health, Galileo was banished to his home near Florence. He went blind in 1637, possibly from damage caused by looking at the sun. Galileo's failing eyesight made him bitter because he could no longer observe the universe. When he died in 1642, he was suffering from arthritis and high blood pressure. Pope Urban VIII refused to forget his feud with Galileo, and Galileo was buried with no ceremony in the Church of Santa Croce in Florence.

1588 English cleric Timothy Bright invents a system of shorthand writing that uses symbols to denote words.

1590 Italian architects Giacomo della Porta and Domenico Fontana complete the vaulting of the dome on St. Peter's Basilica in Rome, designed by Michelangelo.

1586   1588   1590

1585 Flemish mathematician and engineer Simon Stevin, known as Stevinus, introduces decimal fractions into common use.

1588 English cleric William Lee invents a stocking frame, a knitting machine for making hosiery.

The Pendulum Clock

Metal clocks powered by falling weights date from the 1300s, but they were inaccurate. A way to regulate the mechanism was needed, and that arrived in the 1600s.

⟶ The pendulum clock depends on the gradual release of energy from the clock's main spring.

TIMELINE
1590–1600

1590 Dutch optician Zacharias Jansen invents the compound microscope, which has two lenses, one for the eyepiece and one for the objective lens.

1594 Scottish mathematician John Napier devises "natural" logarithms, which he publishes in table form in 1614.

1590   1592   1594

1592 Italian scientist Galileo Galilei makes an air-filled, open-ended, liquid-in-glass thermometer.

KEY:

Astronomy and math

Physical and Life Sciences

Technology

In 1582, the Italian scientist Galileo Galilei showed that a pendulum always swings at a constant rate. He also proved that the rate of swing depends on the length of the pendulum, not on the size of its weight. The time taken for one swing is proportional to the square root of the length of the pendulum. A pendulum 39 inches (99 cm) long takes one second to make one swing (forward and back). If it keeps swinging, it can mark off time.

Galileo instructed his son Vincenzo how to make a clock regulated by a pendulum. Vincenzo did not complete the job, and it was not until 1657 that the first pendulum clock appeared. It was designed by the Dutch scientist Christiaan Huygens and kept time to within five minutes a day, far more accurate than earlier clocks.

The Importance of Temperature

Clock pendulums use a metal rod. However, the length of the rod does not stay the same length. It varies depending on temperature. The rod gets longer when it is warm and shorter when it is cold. A clock with a one-

Timeline

1641 Galileo's pendulum clock design

1656 Huygens' pendulum clock

1726 Graham's mercury pendulum

1728 Harrison's gridiron pendulum

↑ Christiaan Huygens is credited with inventing a practical pendulum clock.

1597 Italian surgeon Gaspare Tagliacozzi practices rhinoplasty (surgery to reshape the nose).

1597 German chemist Andreas Libau prepares hydrochloric acid.

1598 Dutch inventor Cornelis van Drebbel patents a "self-winding" clock.

1596

1598

1600

1596 English writer John Harrington invents a flushing toilet, the water closet (WC).

1599 Flemish engineer and mathematician Stevinus builds a "land yacht," a wind-powered carriage with sails.

The Anchor Escapement

In a mechanical clock, the rate at which power "escapes" from the weight is controlled by a mechanism known as an escapement. An anchor escapement on the pendulum gives a rocking motion to the anchor. It stops and starts the escape wheel, letting it gradually release the power of the falling weight that drives the main wheel.

→ With an anchor escapement, the hour hand of the clock is attached to the axle of the main wheel.

second pendulum, for instance, needs an increase of just 0.0009 inches (0.023 mm) in order to lose about one second a day. A steel rod expands by that much with a rise in temperature of only 4°F (2°C).

Inventors devised ways of making a pendulum of constant length. English inventor George Graham designed the mercury pendulum (announced in 1726), which has a glass jar of mercury as the pendulum's weight. When the pendulum expands because of a rise in temperature, the change is balanced by the upward expansion of the mercury in the jar. Another solution, the gridiron pendulum, was invented by English clockmaker John Harrison in 1728. His design has a grid of alternate brass and steel rods. Brass expands more than steel, so the expansion of the brass

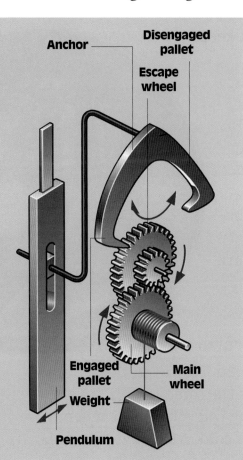

Anchor
Disengaged pallet
Escape wheel
Engaged pallet
Main wheel
Weight
Pendulum

TIMELINE
1600–1610

KEY:

- Astronomy and Math
- Physical and Life Sciences
- Technology

1600 English physician William Gilbert describes the magnetic properties of Earth.

1602 Italian scientist Galileo Galilei formulates the law of falling bodies: that they fall with equal speed regardless of their weight.

1603 Italian anatomist Hieronymus Fabricius ab Aquapendente gives the first clear description of the valves in veins.

1604 German astronomer Johannes Kepler discovers a supernova in the constellation Ophiuchus; it becomes known as Kepler's star.

1600   1602   1604

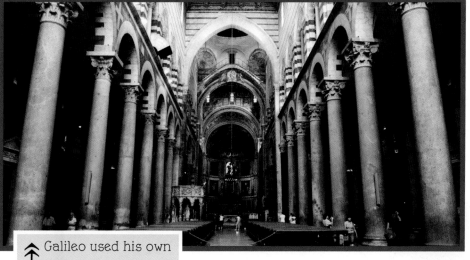

↑ Galileo used his own pulse to time the swinging of a lamp in Pisa Cathedral.

The Constant Pendulum

Galileo noticed that a pendulum has a constant rate of swing. That rate depends on the pendulum's length, not its weight. In mathematical terms, the time of the swing (its period) is proportional to the square root of the length of the pendulum. A longer period needs a longer pendulum.

compensates for the lesser expansion of steel. A pendulum rod made of concentric tubes of iron and zinc achieves a similar result. Today, pendulum rods are made from invar, an alloy of iron and nickel that expands very little when heated.

Have you ever wondered why a grandfather clock is so tall? It has to be long enough to house a 39-inch (99-cm) one-second pendulum, common to all such clocks. They go "tick, tock" every second.

→ The rate of a pendulum's swing depends on the length of the pendulum.

1605 German astronomer Christoph Scheiner invents the pantograph, a device for tracing drawings in order to reduce or enlarge them.

1609 Dutch inventor Cornelis van Drebbel invents an incubator for hens' eggs.

1606

1608

1610

1606 German chemist Andreas Libau writes *Alchymia*, the first modern chemistry textbook.

1608 German-born Dutch lensmaker Hans Lippershey makes a refracting telescope (using two lenses).

1609 Johannes Kepler draws up his first two laws of planetary motion.

The Barometer and Vacuums

In the 1640s, an Italian set out to measure air pressure, caused by the weight of the atmosphere. He proved the existence of the vacuum and invented the barometer.

↑ The famous Magdeburg spheres were, in fact, two hemispheres of copper.

TIMELINE
1610-1620

1610 Italian scientist Galileo Galilei uses the newly invented telescope to observe four of Jupiter's moons and sees craters on the moon.

1612 German astronomer and mathematician Simon Marius publishes the first description of the Andromeda Galaxy.

1614 Italian physician Sanctorius founds the study of the metabolism.

1610

1612

1614

KEY:

Astronomy and Math

Physical and Life Sciences

Technology

1610 French astronomer Nicolas-Claude Fabri de Peiresc discovers the Orion Nebula.

1611 German astronomer Christoph Scheiner observes sunspots (independently of Galileo).

In 1645, Evangelista Torricelli (1608–1647), a mathematician and former assistant to Galileo, took a 6.6-foot (2-m) glass tube, sealed at one end, and filled it with mercury. Keeping his thumb over the open end, he upended the tube in a dish full of mercury and then removed his thumb. Some mercury ran out into the dish, and the mercury level in the tube dropped to about 30 inches (76 cm). What was stopping it all from escaping?

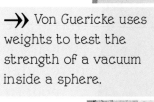

→ Von Guericke uses weights to test the strength of a vacuum inside a sphere.

Atmospheric Pressure

Torricelli reasoned that the weight of the atmosphere (air) pressing on the surface of the mercury in the dish equaled the weight of the mercury left in the tube. The height of the mercury column is therefore a measure of air pressure. The whole device is known as a barometer. Torricelli also noticed that the height of the column varied slightly depending on the weather and deduced that atmospheric pressure must also vary. In 1647, French mathematician René Descartes added a vertical scale to a Torricelli barometer and used it to record weather observations. Pressure is still sometimes measured in inches or millimeters of mercury— "normal" pressure is 30 inches (760 mm).

Timeline

1645 Mercury barometer

1654 Magdeburg spheres

1703 Hawksbee's vacuum pump

1771 Barometer as altimeter

1855 Geissler's vacuum pump

1865 Sprengel's mercury vapor pump

1618 William Oughtred, an English mathematician, introduces the letter "x" in math as the multiplication sign.

1619 English ironmaster Dud Dudley claims to smelt iron using "pit coal" (rather than charcoal). He patents the process two years later.

1616   1618   1620

1617 Scottish mathematician John Napier introduces "Napier's bones," strips of bone or wood that use logarithms to aid calculations.

1620 English mathematician Edmund Gunter introduces the 22-yard (20-m) surveyor's chain, which becomes a standard unit of measurement.

Atmospheric pressure also varies with altitude. The pressure at the top of a mountain is less than that at the foot of the mountain. In 1771, Swiss geologist Jean Deluc began using a sensitive barometer to measure the heights of mountains. A modern altimeter, used in airplanes, is also a modified barometer. Torricelli's barometer was not easy to move around, even if Jean Deluc carried one up mountains. In 1797, a French scientist, Jean Nicolas Fortin (1750–1831), invented a portable mercury barometer.

Understanding Vacuums

In Torricelli's original experiment, what was in the space above the mercury in the closed tube? It was a vacuum, a space in which there is nothing at all. Scientists who wanted to study vacuums needed a way to produce them in the laboratory. In 1654, Otto von Guericke, mayor of Magdeburg, Germany, invented the first air pump, so-called because it was designed to pump air out of a vessel. (Today we would call it a vacuum pump.) He used it to remove the air from between a pair of copper hemispheres, which became held tightly together by the force of atmospheric pressure. Even 16 horses could not pull them apart. Von Guericke's demonstration apparatus became known as the Magdeburg spheres.

Torricelli created the first vacuum. This led to the invention of the barometer and showed that vacuums exist.

TIMELINE
1620–1630

1620 English philosopher Francis Bacon advocates a scientific method of testing a theory by a controlled experiment (hypothesis, experiment, conclusion).

1624 English mathematician Henry Briggs publishes tables to "common" logarithms from 1 to 100,000.

1620   1622   1624

KEY:

Astronomy and Math

Physical and Life Sciences

Technology

1622 English mathematician William Oughtred creates the slide rule, which uses logarithms to perform multiplication and division.

1623 In *Pinax Theatri Botanici*, Swiss botanist Gaspard Bauhin describes 6,000 different plants.

1624 Flemish physician and chemist Jan Baptista van Helmont invents the word "gas."

Torricelli's mercury tube barometer can be replicated today with simple equipment.

More efficient pumps followed. In 1703, English physicist Francis Hawksbee made a vacuum pump that Irish scientist Robert Boyle used to study gases. German physicist Heinrich Geissler used his pump of 1855 to study electrical discharges at low pressures, and 10 years later, German-born British scientist Hermann Sprengel mechanized Geissler's pump. Still used today, it is a mercury vapor pump (or diffusion pump) in which the vapor "captures" molecules of air and carries them away to produce a vacuum. It had important applications, leading to the finding of the rare gases in air, the discovery of the electron, and the invention of the electric lightbulb, among other things.

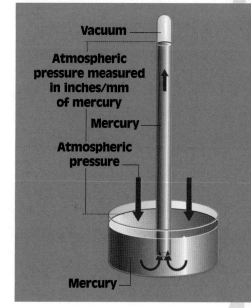

Vacuum

Atmospheric pressure measured in inches/mm of mercury

Mercury

Atmospheric pressure

Mercury

The Mercury Barometer

To re-create Torricelli's original experiment, a closed glass tube is filled with mercury and placed upside down in a dish of mercury. The mercury column in the tube falls slightly, leaving a vacuum in the space above. Atmospheric pressure acting on the mercury in the dish holds up the mercury column. The height of the column above the surface measures the atmospheric pressure.

← The barometer proves and measures atmospheric pressure.

1627 German astronomer Johannes Kepler publishes the *Rudolphine Tables,* describing the motions of the planets.

1628 English physician William Harvey explains the circulation of the blood—the way in which the heart pumps blood through the lungs and around the body.

1626

1628

1630

1626 St. Peter's Basilica in Rome is finally consecrated, having taken 120 years to build.

1629 Italian engineer Giovanni Branca makes a primitive steam turbine.

Isaac Newton

Isaac Newton made fundamental breakthroughs in mathematics and established the basic laws that became the cornerstones of astronomy and physics.

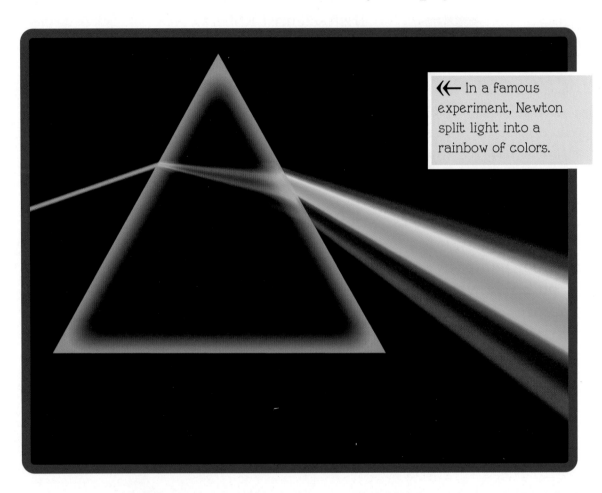

⟵ In a famous experiment, Newton split light into a rainbow of colors.

TIMELINE
1630–1640

1631 English mathematician Thomas Harriot introduces the symbols < and >, meaning "less than" and "more than," respectively.

1633 Italian scientist Galileo Galilei is sentenced to house arrest by the Inquisition for refusing to withdraw his claim that the sun, not Earth, is the center of the universe.

1630   1632   1634

KEY:

Astronomy and Math

Physical and Life Sciences

Technology

1630 Jesuit priests bring to Europe bark of the South American cinchona tree to treat malaria; it is later found to contain the drug quinine.

1631 French astronomer Pierre Gassendi makes the first observation of the transit of the planet Mercury across the sun's disk.

1632 The first modern observatory is built at Leyden (now Leiden) in the Netherlands.

↑ Newton was born in a rural home and spent most of his life outside London.

Isaac Newton was born in a rural area of eastern England. He was brought up by his grandmother and educated at a local school before going to Trinity College (Cambridge University). He received his bachelor's degree from Cambridge in 1665, but was forced to remain in the country town rather than heading into London, as many promising academics did, because of the plague that was raging in the capital at that time. At first, Newton's graduate studies concentrated on mathematics, working out the principles of "fluxions," which were to lead to the development of differential calculus.

Timeline

1642 Newton born in Lincolnshire, England

1665 Binomial theorem (math)

c.1665 Law of gravity and center of gravity

1668 Newton's reflecting telescope

1671 Splits white light into a spectrum

1675 Corpuscular theory of light

1678 Robert Hooke's law of gravity

1687 Book *Principia* published

1703 Newton elected president of the Royal Society

1704 Book *Opticks* published

1705 Newton is knighted

1727 Dies in London

1638 English astronomer William Gascoigne and Frenchman Adrien Auzout independently invent the eyepiece micrometer, which enables accurate measurements to be made with telescopes and microscopes.

1639 English astronomers William Crabtree and Jeremiah Horrocks make the first observation of the transit of Venus across the sun's disk.

1636   1638   1640

1637 French mathematician René Descartes introduces analytic geometry, a way to use algebraic equations to represent geometric lines and curves.

1639 A glassworks set up in Plymouth, Maryland, is one of the first "factories" in Britain's American colonies.

↑ Newton studied at Trinity College, Cambridge, and became a professor there.

The First Theories

In 1667, Newton received a fellowship from Trinity College, where he became professor of mathematics in 1669. He turned his attention to what happens when objects move—what makes them start moving and what stops them. His conclusions are summed up in Newton's three laws of motion (see page 36). All of the laws can be observed by watching a game of pool, although you do not have to be a physicist to play it!

Newton's next contribution was to have a profound effect on astronomy. According to the well-known story—which probably never happened—he was sitting in an orchard when he saw an apple fall. (In some versions of the story, the apple even fell on his head.) Why did the apple fall? Whatever prompted his investigations, Newton concluded that the apple must be attracted to Earth by a force, which we now call the force of gravity. He also deduced that every object behaves as if its mass were concentrated in one place, its center of gravity (now called the center of mass). Applying his own laws of motion, he figured out that all objects in

TIMELINE 1640–1650

1640 French mathematician Pierre de Fermat proposes Fermat's principle: light always travels in a straight line.

1642 French scientist Blaise Pascal builds a wooden mechanical calculating machine—it is an early step towards a computer.

1642 German anatomist Johann Wirsung discovers the pancreatic duct, which carries digestive juices to the duodenum.

1640   1642   1644

1641 Dutch naturalist Nicolaas Tulp describes a chimpanzee brought to the Netherlands; the chimpanzee was the first of the great apes to be discovered.

1642 Pascal proposes Pascal's law, which states that the pressure within a liquid is the same everywhere. The principle underlies all hydraulic machinery.

KEY:

Astronomy and Math

Physical and Life Sciences

Technology

the universe are affected by such gravitational forces—it is gravity that keeps the moon in orbit around Earth and Earth in orbit around the sun. He produced a formula, the universal law of gravitation, that states the gravitational force between any two objects—whether they are two pool balls or two stars—is equal to the product of their masses and inversely proportional to the distance between them. The English scientist Robert Hooke also devised a law of gravity in about 1678 and published his ideas a few years later. This led to a bitter dispute between the two great men.

Optical Studies

In the branch of physics we now call optics, Newton's main studies concerned the nature of light. By allowing a narrow beam of white light from the sun to pass

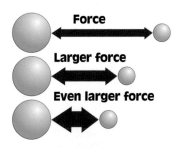

The force of gravity is inversely proportional to distance: the closer together, the larger the force

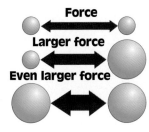

The force of gravity is proportional to the product of the masses: the larger the masses, the larger the force

Newton's laws explained the force of gravity in terms of distance and mass.

Newton's Law of Gravity

Isaac Newton formulated his law of gravity to deal with the attractive force (gravitation) that exists between any two objects that have mass. The strength of the force depends on how close the two objects are (the nearer they are, the stronger is the force trying to pull them together) and how massive they are (the more massive they are, the stronger the force between them—we don't notice the pull of smaller objects). In mathematical terms, the gravitational force is proportional to the product of the masses and inversely proportional to the distance between them.

1645 English physician Daniel Whistler first diagnoses the childhood disease rickets.

1647 French scientist Blaise Pascal builds a primitive version of the roulette wheel to test his ideas on probability.

1646

1648

1650

1645 Italian physicist Evangelista Torricelli constructs the first mercury barometer.

1646 The English scientist Thomas Browne coins the word "electricity" (which at the time referred only to static electricity).

1649 English physician Henry Power discovers the extremely narrow capillary blood vessels.

Newton's Laws of Motion

In addition to his law of gravity, Newton also formulated laws about another major area of physics: motion. Newton's first law of motion states that an object at rest will remain at rest (and a moving object will continue moving) unless an outside force acts on it. According to Newton's second law, force can be defined as something that makes an object accelerate (force equals mass times acceleration). The third law states that for every "action" (a force that one object exerts on another) there is an equal and opposite "reaction" (exerted by the second object on the first).

↑ All three of Newton's laws of motion can be seen during a game of pool.

through a glass prism—whose angles caused the light to refract, or bend—Newton split the light into a multicolored spectrum, the sequence of colors seen in a rainbow. He showed that white light is actually made up of a variety of colors. (Today we say that it is made up of many different wavelengths.)

Telescopes of the time often produced images that were surrounded by a spectrum of colors because the poor-quality lenses brought different colors into focus in different places. Newton overcame the problem by using mirrors instead of lenses to focus the image. In 1668, he produced one of the first reflecting telescopes with mirrors he made himself.

TIMELINE
1650–1660

1650 German scholar Athanasius Kircher demonstrates that sound does not travel in a vacuum.

1650 The first properly equipped chemistry laboratory is established at the University of Leyden (now Leiden) in the Netherlands.

1653 French scientist Blaise Pascal devises Pascal's triangle, in which each number is the sum of the two numbers above it.

1650   1652   1654

KEY:

Astronomy and Math

Physical and Life Sciences

Technology

1650 German inventor Stephen Farfler constructs a three-wheeled chair, an early wheelchair.

1652 Dutch hydraulic engineer Cornelius Vermuyden drains the Fens, a large marsh region in eastern England.

1654 German physicist Otto von Guericke invents an air pump (vacuum pump).

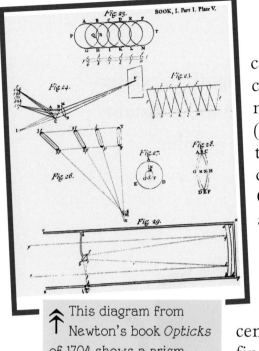

This diagram from Newton's book *Opticks* of 1704 shows a prism splitting a ray of white light into a spectrum.

Newton was convinced that light is composed of a "flux" of minute particles ("corpuscles"). The theory was soon challenged by Christiaan Huygens and others, who suggested that light instead travels as waves. The argument raged until the 20th century, when physicists finally concluded that light has properties of both particles and waves; but this realization had to await the development of quantum theory.

In 1703, Newton was elected president of the Royal Society, and two years later he was knighted (the first scientist to receive the honor). As Sir Isaac Newton, he continued to be showered with honors. His final tribute was a state funeral and burial in Westminster Abbey, London. His name lives on in the SI unit of force, which is called the newton (the force that gives 1 kilogram an acceleration of 1 meter per second per second).

The title page of Newton's 1704 book, which created the modern science of optics, or the study of light.

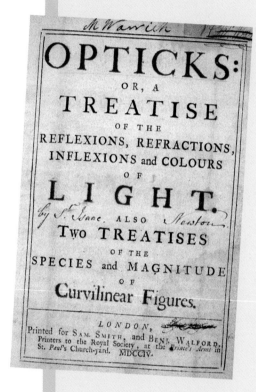

1655 Dutch scientist Christiaan Huygens uses a homemade telescope to observe the rings around the planet Saturn.

1656 Dutch scientist Christiaan Huygens invents a pendulum clock.

1657 Huygens writes the first book on mathematical probability theory.

1658 English scientist Robert Hooke makes a watch regulated by a hairspring, which releases the power of the main spring very gradually.

1659 Swiss mathematician Johann Rahn introduces the division sign (÷) to math.

1656   1658   1660

Telescopes

The first lenses were used mainly as magnifying glasses. But scientists and astronomers needed to see distant objects. The telescope made this possible.

← Isaac Newton built his reflecting telescope in 1668; it magnified objects about 40 times.

TIMELINE
1660–1670

1661 Irish scientist Robert Boyle defines chemical elements for the first time.

1662 Boyle formulates Boyle's law, which states that at a fixed temperature, the pressure of a gas is inversely proportional to its volume.

1665 Robert Hooke proposes the wave theory of light, later championed by Christiaan Huygens.

1660   1662   1664

1661 Dutch scientist Christiaan Huygens invents the manometer, a device for measuring gas pressure.

1664 English scientist Robert Hooke proposes that the planets are held in their orbits by the gravity of the sun.

1665 Hooke coins the word "cell" to describe the "little boxes" he sees in plant tissue through a microscope.

KEY:

- Astronomy and Math
- Physical and Life Sciences
- Technology

Hans Lippershey, the German-born Dutch eyeglass maker, made his first telescope in 1608. He sold his invention to the Dutch government for use by the military. News of the device reached the Italian scientist Galileo Galilei, who immediately made his own telescopes to study the heavens. Among his discoveries were sunspots, craters on the moon, and the four major moons of Jupiter.

Improving the View

In 1611, German Christoph Scheiner made a telescope that provided a wider field of view by using two convex lenses. Called an astronomical telescope, it produces an upside-down image. For centuries afterward, images of the moon, for instance, were always shown with "north" at the bottom.

Lenses of the time suffered from defects such as chromatic aberration, in which a fringe of color surrounded an image. They could be improved by grinding and polishing lenses.

<< This monument at the Griffith Park Observatory in Los Angeles shows the astronomical pioneers Johannes Kepler, Galileo Galilei, and Nicolaus Copernicus.

Timeline

1608 First refracting telescope

1655 Huygens' improved refractor

1663 Gregory's reflecting telescope

1668 Newton's reflecting telescope

1672 Cassegrain's improved reflector

1758 Dollond's achromatic telescope

1666 French engineer Jean de Thévenot invents the spirit level.

1666 Italian astronomer Giovanni Cassini observes the polar ice caps on Mars.

1669 German alchemist Hennig Brand discovers phosphorus in urine; it is the first discovery of a new element since ancient times.

1666   1668   1670

1665 The first blood transfusion, carried out by English physician Richard Lower, takes place between two dogs.

1668 English mathematician John Wallis proposes the law of conservation of momentum: the momentum of objects before a collision is the same as their combined momentum afterward.

Refracting and Reflecting Telescopes

One kind of refracting telescope is the type originally designed by Galileo in 1609 (top). It uses two lenses and produces an upright image. Small versions can be paired to form binoculars. Of the two reflecting designs shown beneath, the Newtonian has the eyepiece at the side, which can be inconvenient in a large telescope. The Cassegrainian telescope has the eyepiece at the lower end, where it is easier to use.

⟩⟩ The arrangement of lenses and mirrors in refracting and reflecting telescopes.

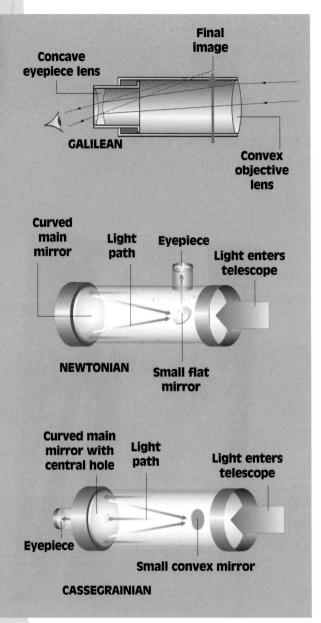

Final image

Concave eyepiece lens

GALILEAN

Convex objective lens

Curved main mirror

Light path

Eyepiece

Light enters telescope

NEWTONIAN

Small flat mirror

Curved main mirror with central hole

Light path

Light enters telescope

Eyepiece

CASSEGRAINIAN

Small convex mirror

But it was not until 1758 that Englishman John Dollond made an achromatic telescope. His method, still used today, involves making a compound lens with two components stuck together. The second component, made of crown glass, corrects the aberrations caused by the first component, which is made out of flint glass. It works because the two types of glass bend light rays in slightly different ways.

Another method of avoiding chromatic aberration involved using lenses with slight curvature and therefore a long focal length (the distance from the main mirror or object lens to the eyepiece). This

TIMELINE
1670–1680

1670 French winemaker Dom Pérignon creates champagne.

1673 Dutch scientist Antonie van Leeuwenhoek begins describing his observations of microscopic creatures.

1674 English glassmaker George Ravenscroft develops lead crystal glass.

1670

1672

1674

KEY:

Astronomy and Math

Physical and Life Sciences

Technology

1670 By measuring part of the meridian (a line of longitude), French astronomer Jean Picard makes it possible to calculate the accurate circumference of Earth.

1671 English scientist Isaac Newton uses a glass prism to split white light into a spectrum of colors.

1675 The Royal Greenwich Observatory is completed near London; it gives its name to the Greenwich Meridian (at longitude 0°).

meant making telescopes very long. Telescopes measuring 33 feet (10 m) long were common.

Mirrors Instead of Lenses

These early telescopes were refracting telescopes. A better way to view images is with a reflecting telescope that uses mirrors instead of lenses, because mirrors do not cause chromatic aberration. James Gregory, a Scottish mathematician, realized this in 1663 when he published a design for a telescope that had a small, curved secondary mirror to reflect the light back through a hole in the primary mirror to an eyepiece. English scientist Robert Hooke later improved the design. Other types of reflecting telescopes were built—by English scientist Isaac Newton in 1668 and by French priest Laurent Cassegrain in 1672. (The Cassegrainian design was not perfected until 1740 by Scottish optician James Short.) In 1857, French physicist Léon Foucault devised a method of silvering glass to make curved mirrors. They were easier to manufacture, and could be resilvered if accidentally damaged. Since then, telescopes have been made larger and more powerful—it is far easier to make a big mirror than it is to make a big lens.

⬆ William Herschel's 1794 reflecting telescope was 20 feet (6 m) long.

1675 Isaac Newton proposes (but does not publish) the corpuscular theory, that light travels in a series of minute particles.

1676 Danish astronomer Ole Rømer attempts unsuccessfully to measure the speed of light.

1676   1678   1680

1676 Van Leeuwenhoek reports his observations of bacteria through a simple, homemade microscope.

1676 Irish scientist Robert Boyle invents the hydrometer, for measuring the relative density of a liquid.

1679 German mathematician Gottfried Leibniz introduces binary arithmetic, which uses only two digits: today is it used by all computers.

The Nature of Light

Does light consist of a stream of minute particles, like bullets from a machine gun? Or does it consist of waves capable of rippling across the vast vacuum of space?

⟫ Archimedes may have used a lens to defend Syracuse against naval attack.

TIMELINE
1680-1690

1681 On the island of Mauritius in the Indian Ocean, the flightless dodo (*Raphus cucullatus*) is hunted to extinction.

1682 English botanist Nehemiah Grew describes the male and female parts of flowers.

1684 Japanese mathematician Seki Kowa introduces the use of determinants to math; they are useful for solving simultaneous equations.

1680   1682   1684

KEY:

Astronomy and Math

Physical and Life Sciences

Technology

1680 Irish scientist Robert Boyle invents a match that uses a mixture of sulfur and phosphorus; it remains the basic match for over 200 years.

1682 English astronomer Edmund Halley plots the course of the comet now named for him.

Fermat saw that shadows are formed because light travels in straight lines.

Rays of light bend as they go through a lens and come to a focus. Concentrating the rays allows a magnifying glass to be used as a burning glass. In 212 B.C., Greek scientist Archimedes is said to have used a burning glass to destroy Roman ships attacking Syracuse.

In 1621, the Dutch mathematician Willebrord Snell measured this bending of light. Another mathematician, the Frenchman Pierre de Fermat, figured out how light casts shadows. He stated that it is because light always travels in straight lines—it will not "go around corners" to illuminate a shadow. Known as Fermat's principle, it was proposed in 1640. He also observed that light travels more slowly through a denser medium.

Timeline

1621 Snell's law (refraction of light)

1640 Fermat's principle

1665 Wave theory (Hooke)

1675 Corpuscular theory (Newton)

1676 Speed of light (Rømer)

1801 Interference of light

1900 Quantum theory (Planck)

1924 Wave-particle duality

1687 English scientist Isaac Newton publishes his major work *Principia*, in which he sets out theories in astronomy, math, and physics.

1687 German astronomer Gottfried Kirch discovers that Zeta Cygni is a variable star.

1686   1688   1690

1686 English naturalist John Ray proposes the word "species" to describe an interbreeding group of plants.

1687 French physicist Guillaume Amontons invents a hygrometer, for measuring the humidity of the atmosphere.

1689 In Germany, Johann Denner develops the clarinet.

Snell's Law

Snell's law is named for Willebrord Snell, the Dutch mathematician who discovered it in 1621. It concerns refraction, or how a ray of light changes direction when it goes from one transparent medium to another, such as moving from air into a block of glass. The amount of refraction depends on a property of the denser medium, called its refractive index.

⟫ The refractive index of glass is the relationship between the angle of incidence and the angle of refraction.

The Speed of Light

The first attempt to measure the speed of light was made in 1676 by Danish astronomer Ole Rømer. He was checking predictions about the timing of eclipses of Jupiter's moons (when they move out of sight behind the planet). Rømer discovered that the eclipses seemed to happen earlier than predicted when Earth was moving toward Jupiter and later when Earth was moving away from it. He accounted for the differences by assuming that the light had to travel a shorter or longer distance, and that light must therefore have a finite speed, which he calculated as 140,000 miles (225,000 km) per second—about 75 percent of the actual value. It was nearly 200 years before French physicist Armand Fizeau obtained a more accurate value of 195,737 miles (315,000 km) per second. The value that is used today is 186,288 miles (299,793 km) per second.

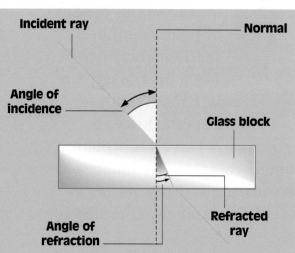

Incident ray — Normal — Angle of incidence — Glass block — Angle of refraction — Refracted ray

What Is Light?

In 1675, English scientist Isaac Newton postulated that light travels as a stream of minute particles

TIMELINE 1690-1700

1690 English naturalist John Ray distinguishes between plants with one seed leaf (monocotyledons) and those with two (dicotyledons).

1694 English clockmaker Daniel Quare makes a portable barometer.

1694 Italian scientist Carlo Renaldini suggests that the freezing and boiling points of water should be used as fixed points on thermometers.

1690 — 1692 — 1694

1691 John Ray suggests that fossils are the remains of creatures that lived in the distant past.

1692 The Canal du Midi is completed in France, linking the Atlantic Ocean and the Mediterranean Sea.

KEY:
- Astronomy and Math
- Physical and Life Sciences
- Technology

("corpuscles"). Various physicists challenged this idea, the first being Robert Hooke, who had already proposed the wave theory in 1665. The final nail in the coffin of the corpuscular theory came in 1801, when English physicist Thomas Young discovered the interference of light. He found that white light shining through a narrow slit is split into the colors of the rainbow. At that time it could be explained only if light was assumed to travel as waves.

The wave theory was assumed to be correct until the beginning of the 20th century, when German physicist Max Planck put forward his quantum theory. It postulates that all forms of energy, including light, travel in finite "packets," or quanta, similar to Newton's corpuscles. But in 1924, French physicist Louis de Broglie put forward the idea that moving particles can also behave like waves, as was soon proved true. So it turned out that everyone had been correct—and one of the great arguments of science melted away.

↓ Isaac Newton believed that light travels as a stream of particles.

1697 German chemist George Stahl champions the (incorrect) phlogiston theory (that burning objects release a gas, phlogiston).

1698 English mining engineer Thomas Savery invents a steam pump, the forerunner of the atmospheric steam engine.

1696

1698

1700

1696 Dutch scientist Antonie van Leeuwenhoek describes "animalcules"—microorganisms today known as protists.

1698 The first lighthouse is built on Eddystone Rocks in the English Channel.

1699 English botanist John Woodward demonstrates that plants grow best if other substances are added to their water as nutrients.

Glossary

anatomy The scientific study of the human body.

astronomy The study of objects outside Earth's atmosphere.

concave Describes a lens that is thicker at its edges and thinner toward its center.

convex Describes a lens that bulges outward toward its center.

differential calculus An advanced branch of math.

experiment A controlled practical exercise carried out in order to test a scientific hypothesis.

geometry The study of shapes and volume.

gravity The force of attraction that exists between all objects, but usually referring to the hold of planets and other heavenly bodies.

Inquisition A religious court set up by the Catholic church to enforce church doctrines.

lens A piece of glass that has been ground to focus beams of light together or to separate them.

movable type Wooden or metal letters that can be assembled into words, sentences, and pages for printing, then taken apart and reused.

observatory A building that houses astronomical instruments such as telescopes.

optics The scientific study of light.

reflection The angle at which a beam of light is reflected from another surface.

Reformation A period of religious reform and conflict that followed Martin Luther's criticisms of the Catholic church in 1517 and the creation of the Protestant church.

refraction The angle at which a beam of light changes direction when it passes from one medium to another, such as from air into glass.

Renaissance A period in European history from about 1350 to about 1550, marked by renewed interest in the Classical learning of ancient Greece and Rome.

transit A phenomenon in which one astronomical body passes in front of another, such as a planet passing in front of the sun.

Further Reading

Books

Anderson, Margaret J. *Isaac Newton: The Greatest Scientist of All Time.* Berkeley Heights, NJ: Enslow Publishers, 2008.

Boerst, William J. *Isaac Newton: Organizing the Universe.* Greensboro, NC: Morgan Reynolds Publishing, 2004.

Burns, William E. *The Scientific Revolution: An Encyclopedia.* Santa Barbara, CA: ABC-Clio, 2001.

Childress, Diana. *Johannes Gutenberg and the Printing Press.* Minneapolis, MN: Twenty-First Century Books, 2007.

Hilliam, Rachel. *Galileo: Father of Modern Science.* New York: Rosen Publishing Group, 2004.

McNeese, Tim. *Galileo: Renaissance Scientist and Astronomer.* Philadelphia, PA: Chelsea House, 2005.

Mullins, Lisa. *Science in the Renaissance.* New York: Crabtree Publishing Company, 2009.

Reed, Jennifer. *Leonardo da Vinci: Genius of Art and Science.* Berkeley Heights, NJ: Enslow Publishers, 2004.

Rees, Fran. *Johannes Gutenberg: Inventor of the Printing Press.* Minneapolis, MN: Compass Point Books, 2006.

Somervill, Barbara A. *Nicolaus Copernicus: Father of Modern Astronomy.* Minneapolis: Compass Point Books, 2005.

Web Sites

http://www.mos.org/sln/Leonardo//
The Museum of Science "Exploring Leonardo" web site.

http://www.scienceandyou.org/articles/ess_15.shtml
Science and You page on science during the Renaissance.

http://library.thinkquest.org/26220/astronomers/renaissance_astronomers.html
Think Quest's biographies of Renaissance astronomers.

http://www.newton.ac.uk/newton.html
Resources about Isaac Newton from the Isaac Newton Institute of Mathematical Sciences.

http://inventors.about.com/od/gstartinventors/a/Gutenberg.htm
About.com page on Johannes Gutenberg and the invention of the printing press.

Index